Look After Pets

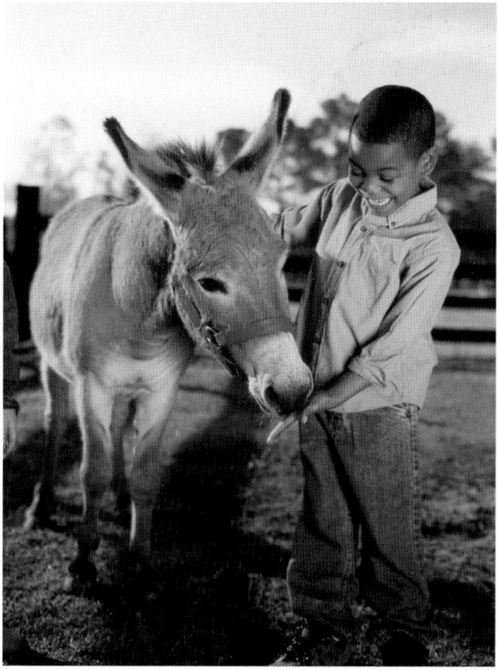

written by Pam Holden

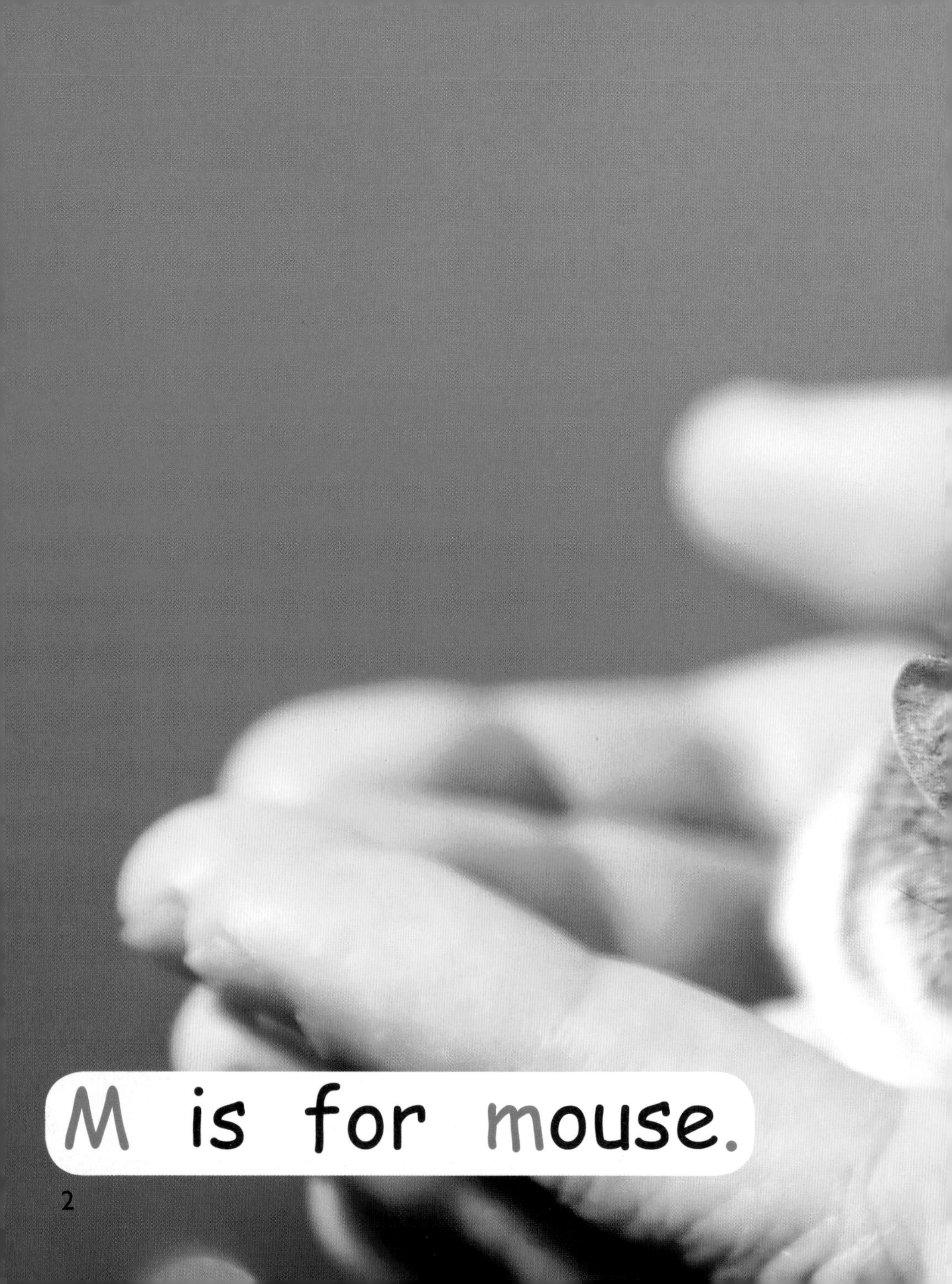

M is for mouse.

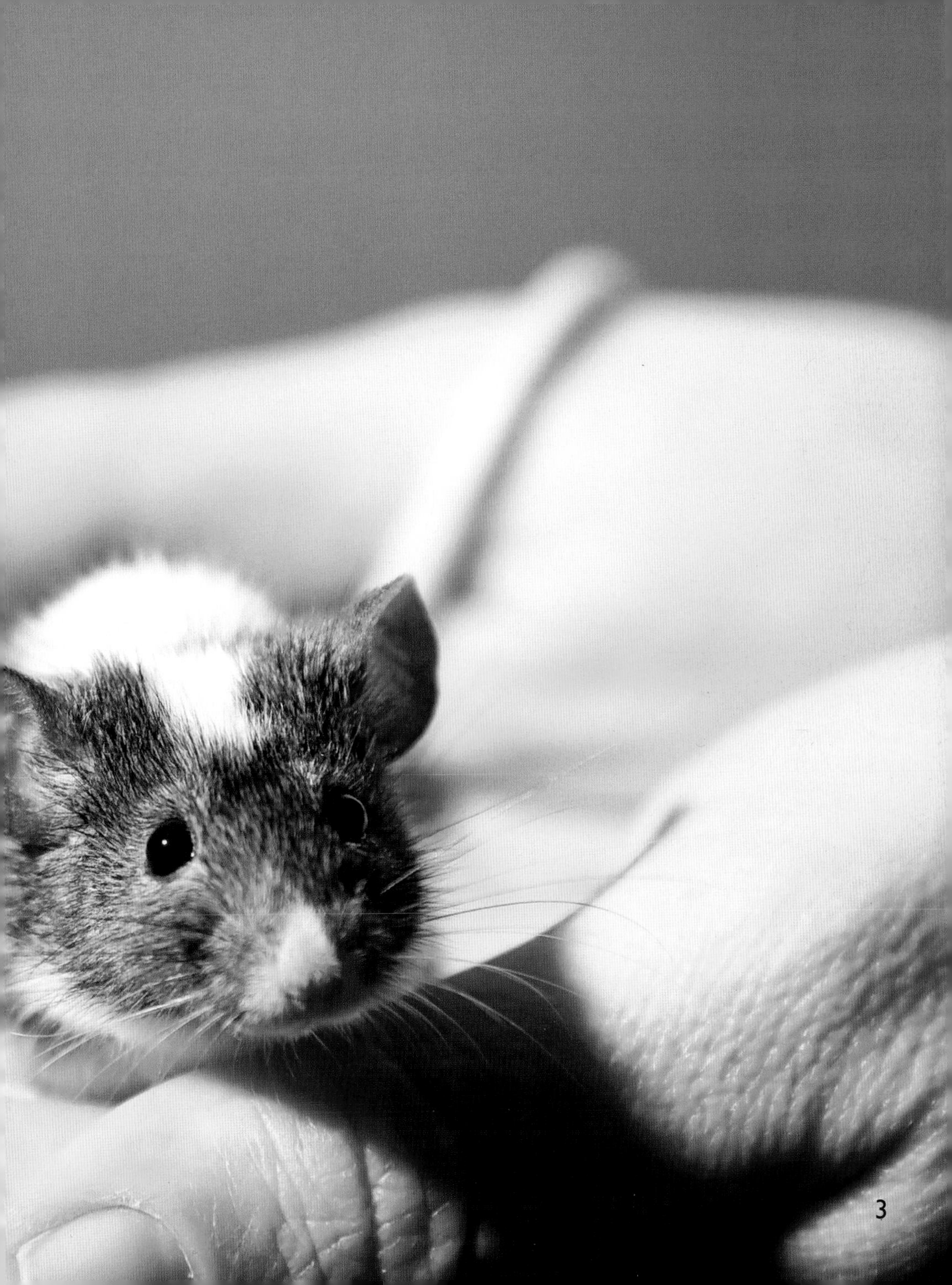

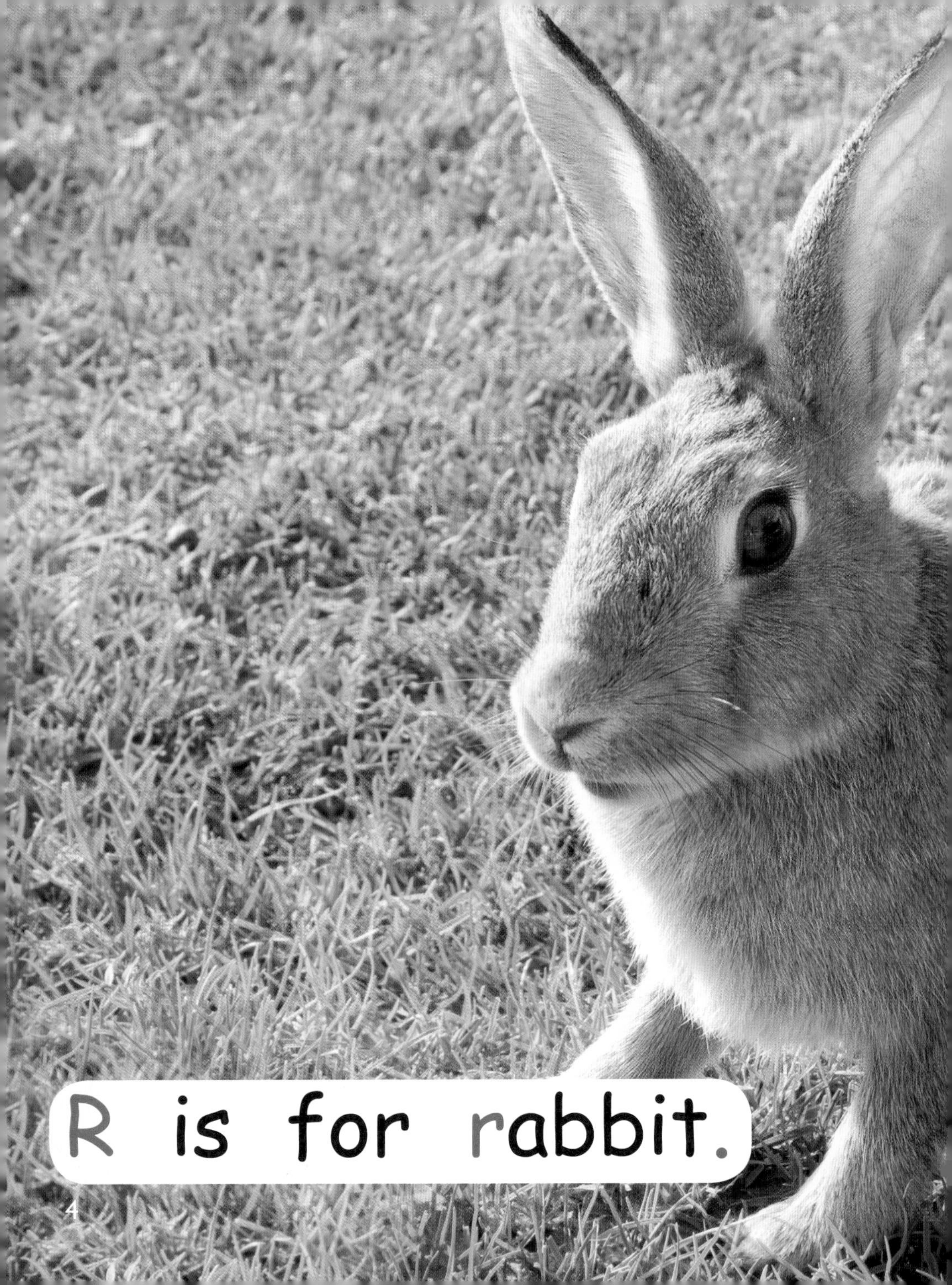

R is for rabbit.

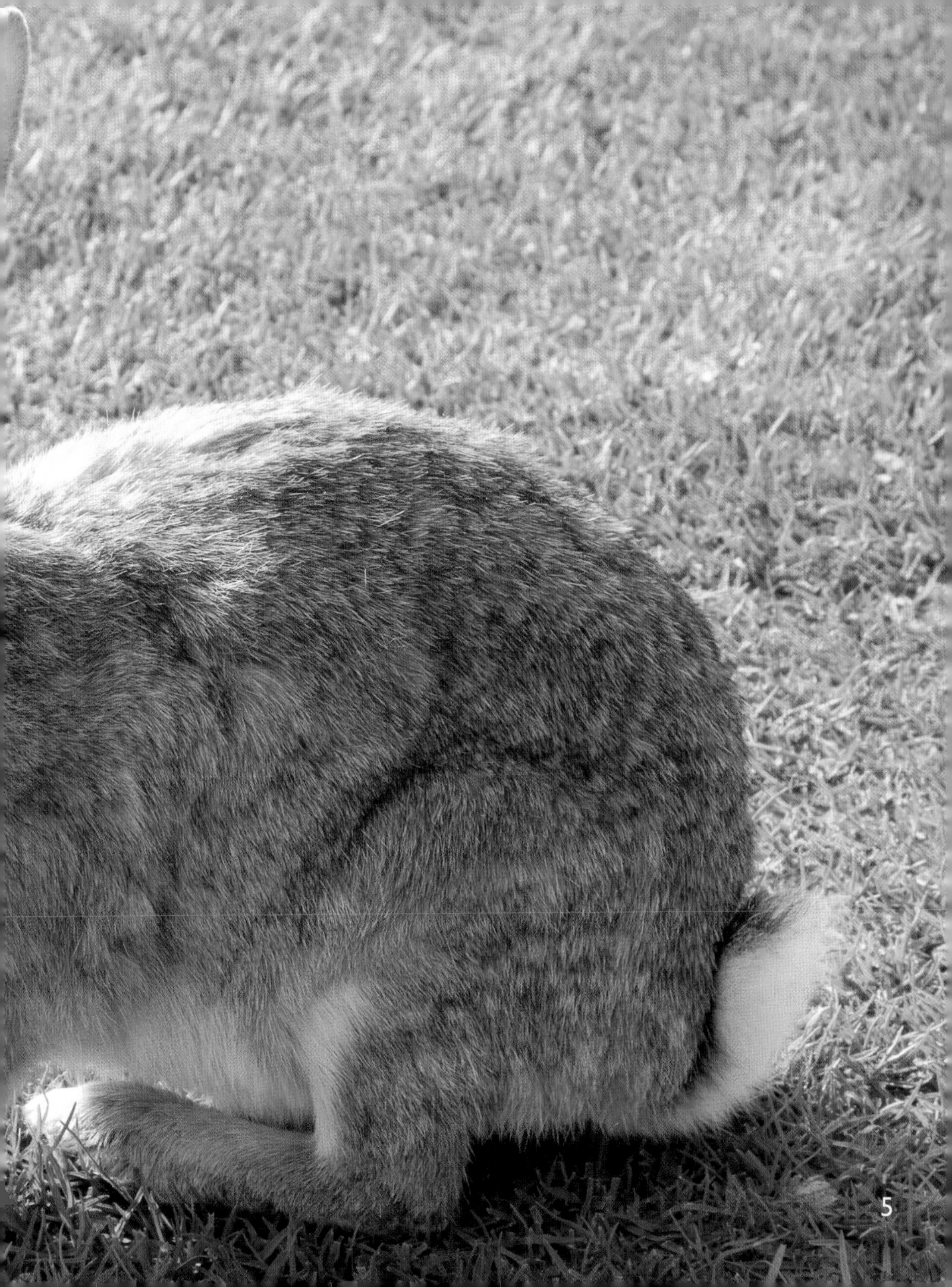

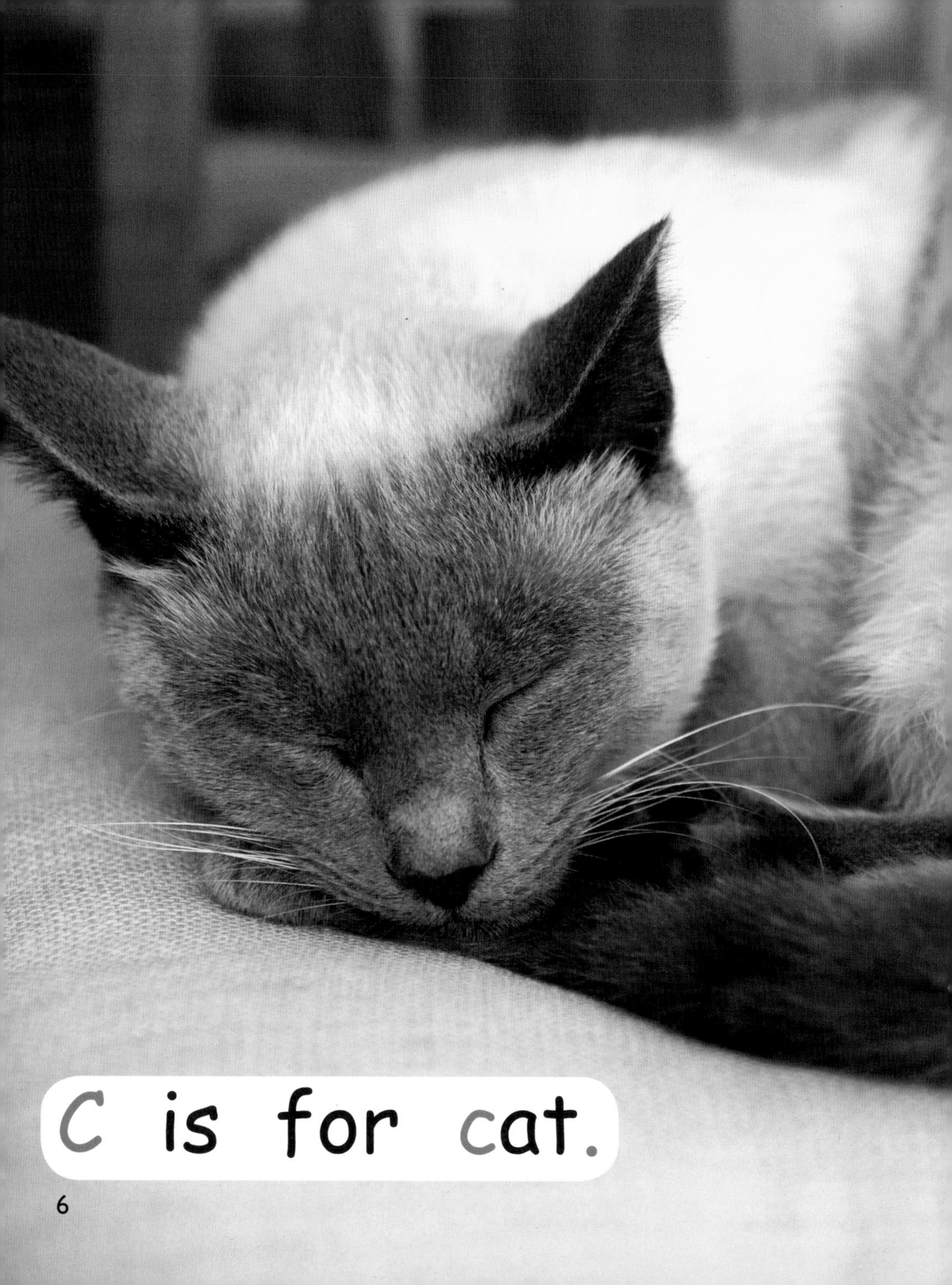

C is for cat.

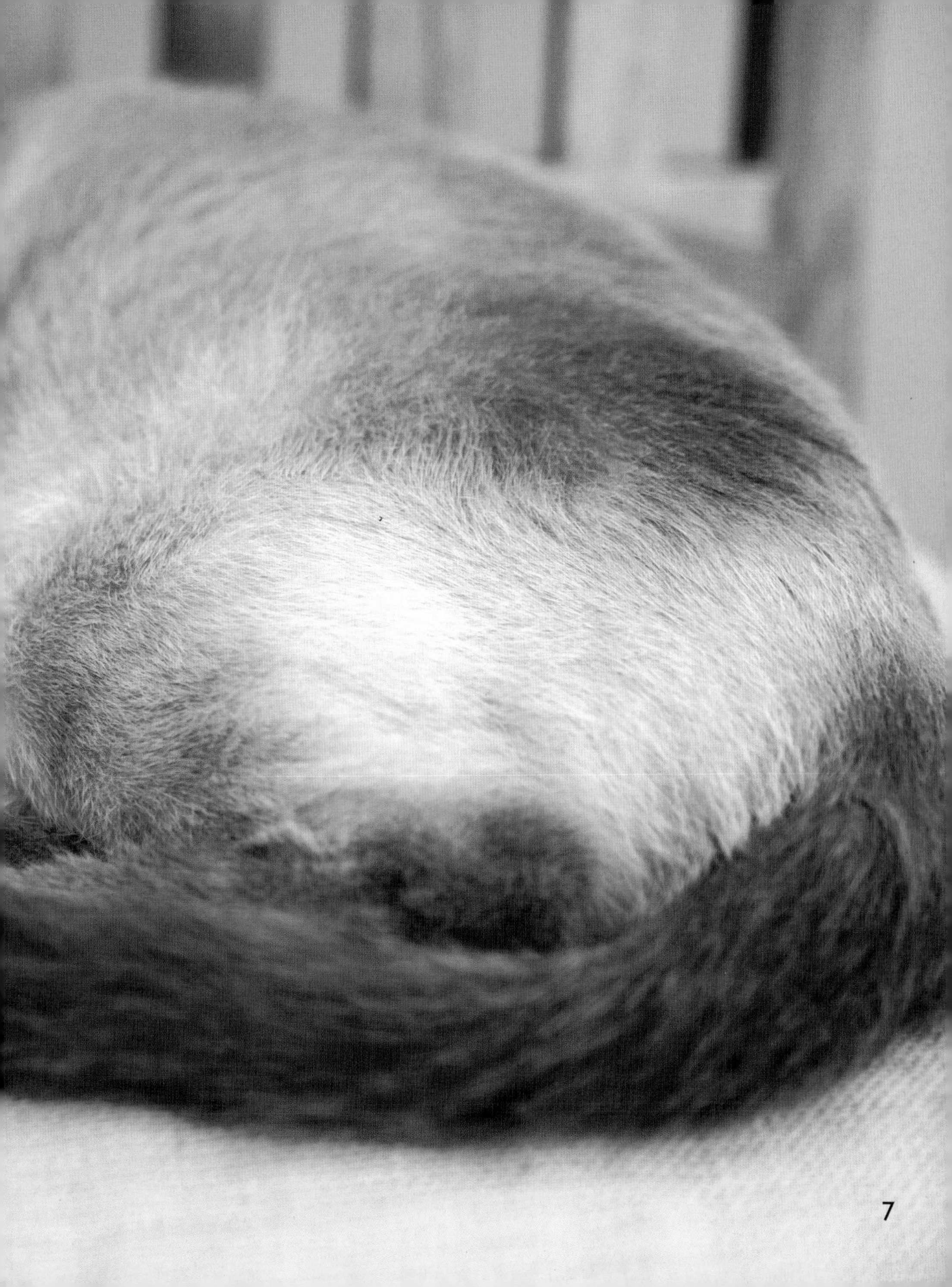

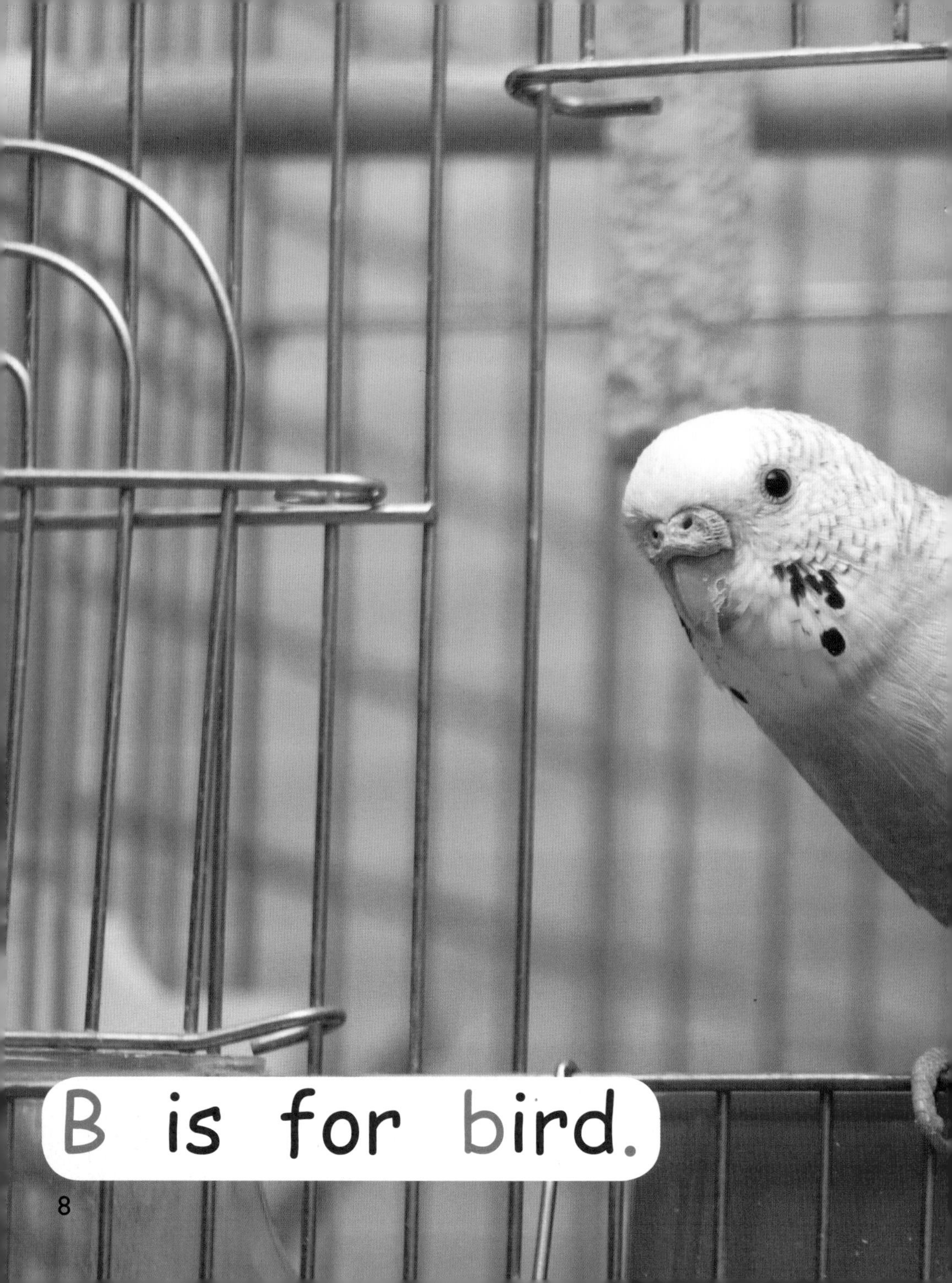

B is for bird.

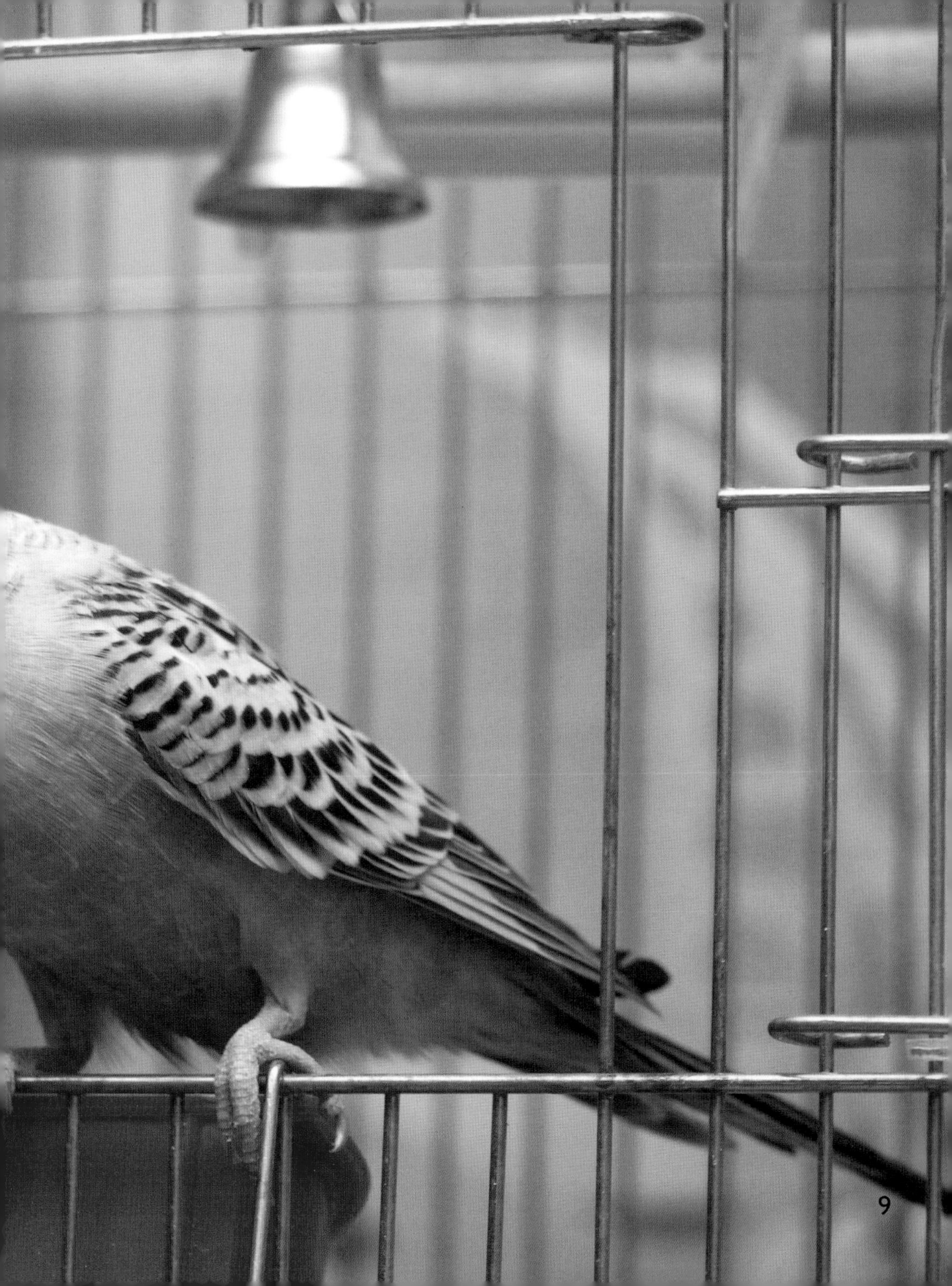

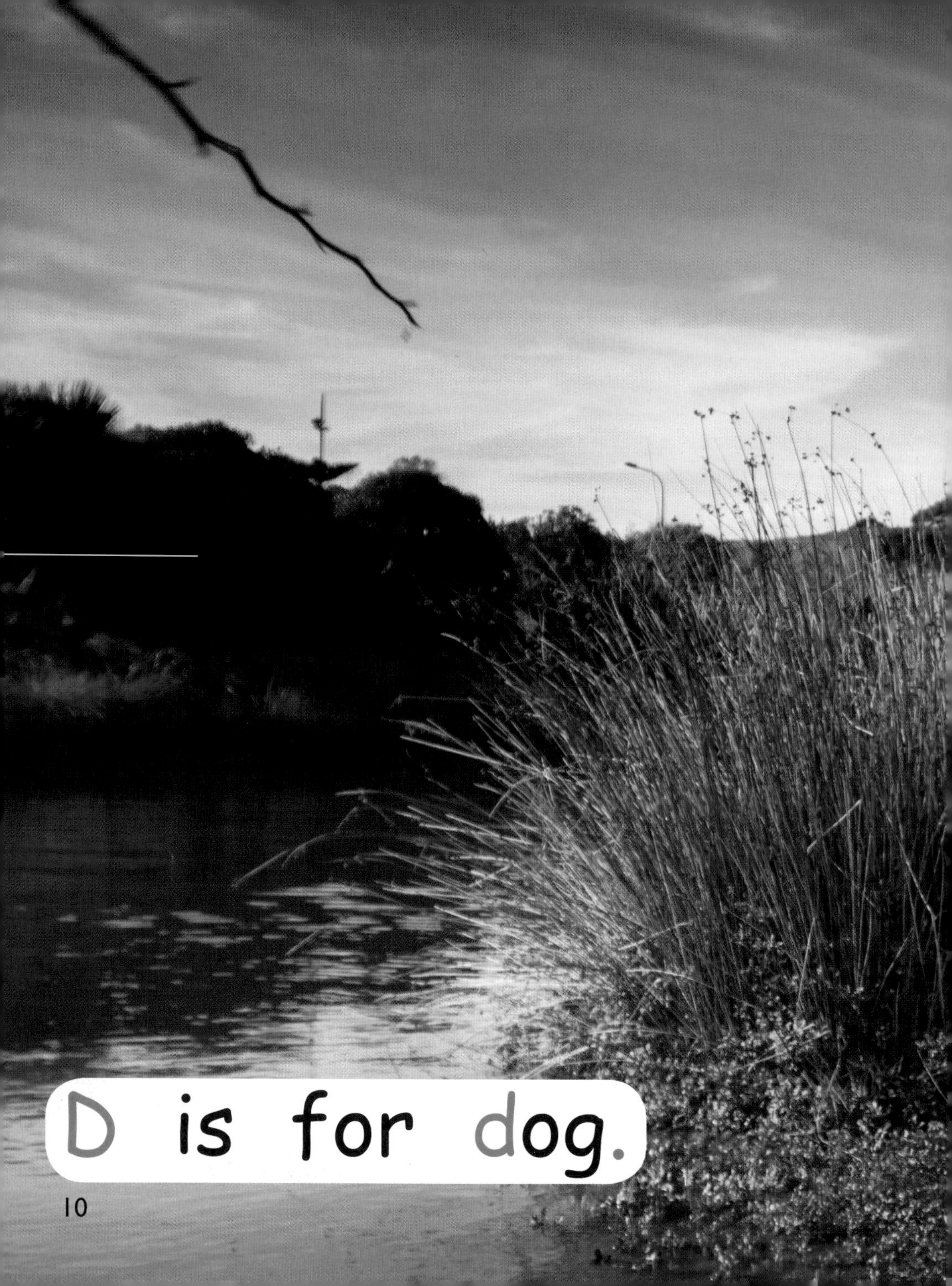

D is for dog.

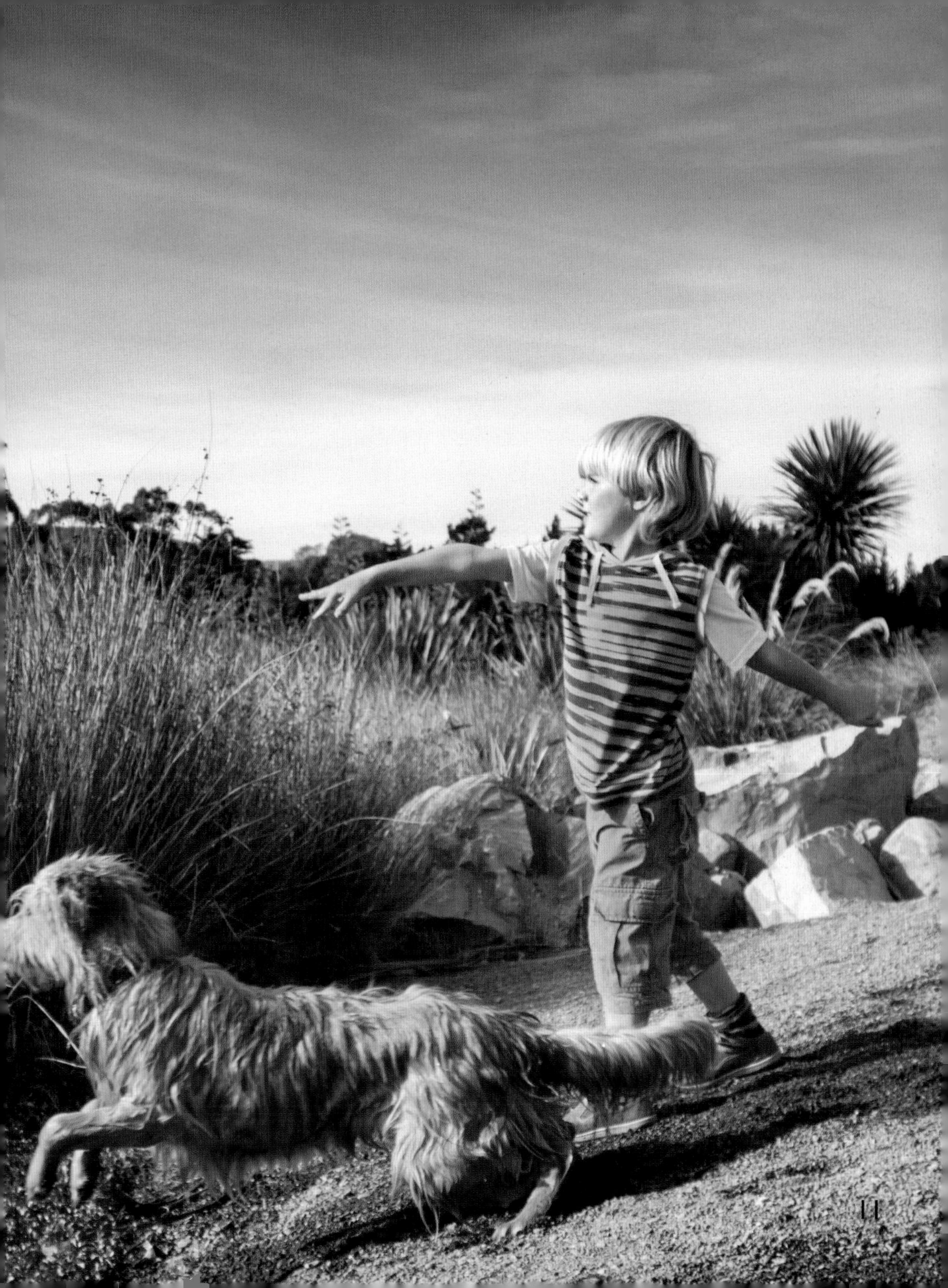

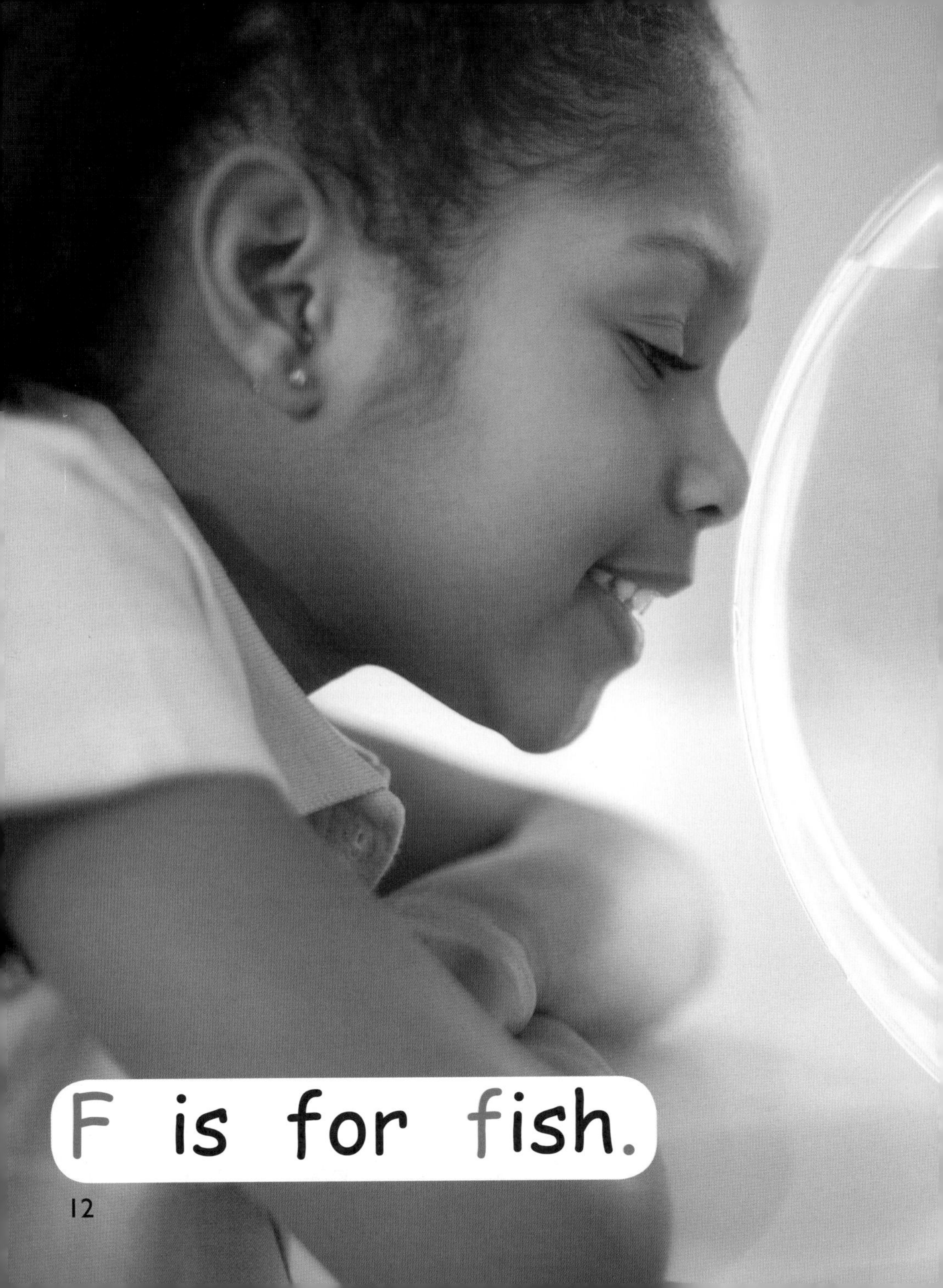

F is for fish.

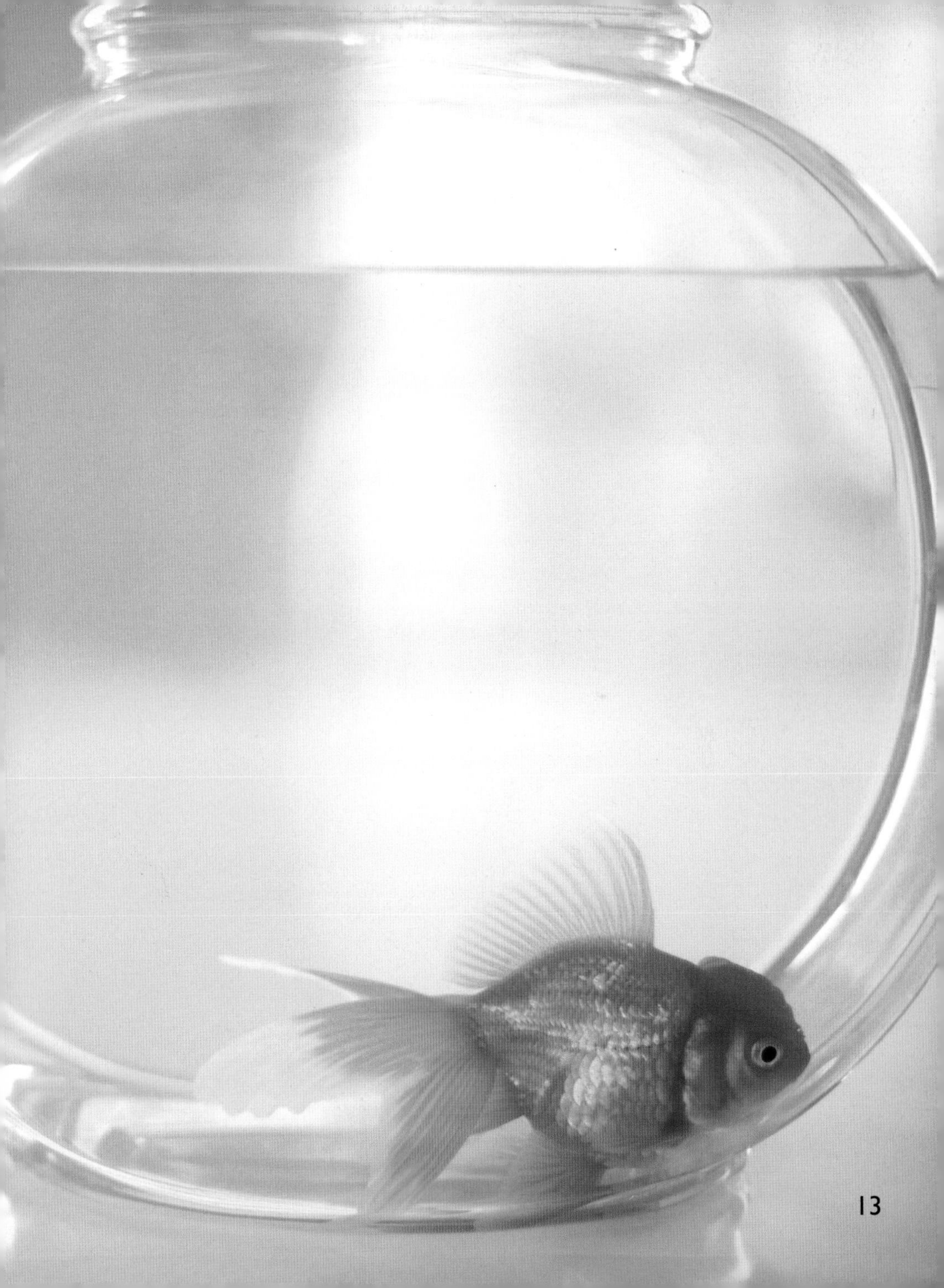

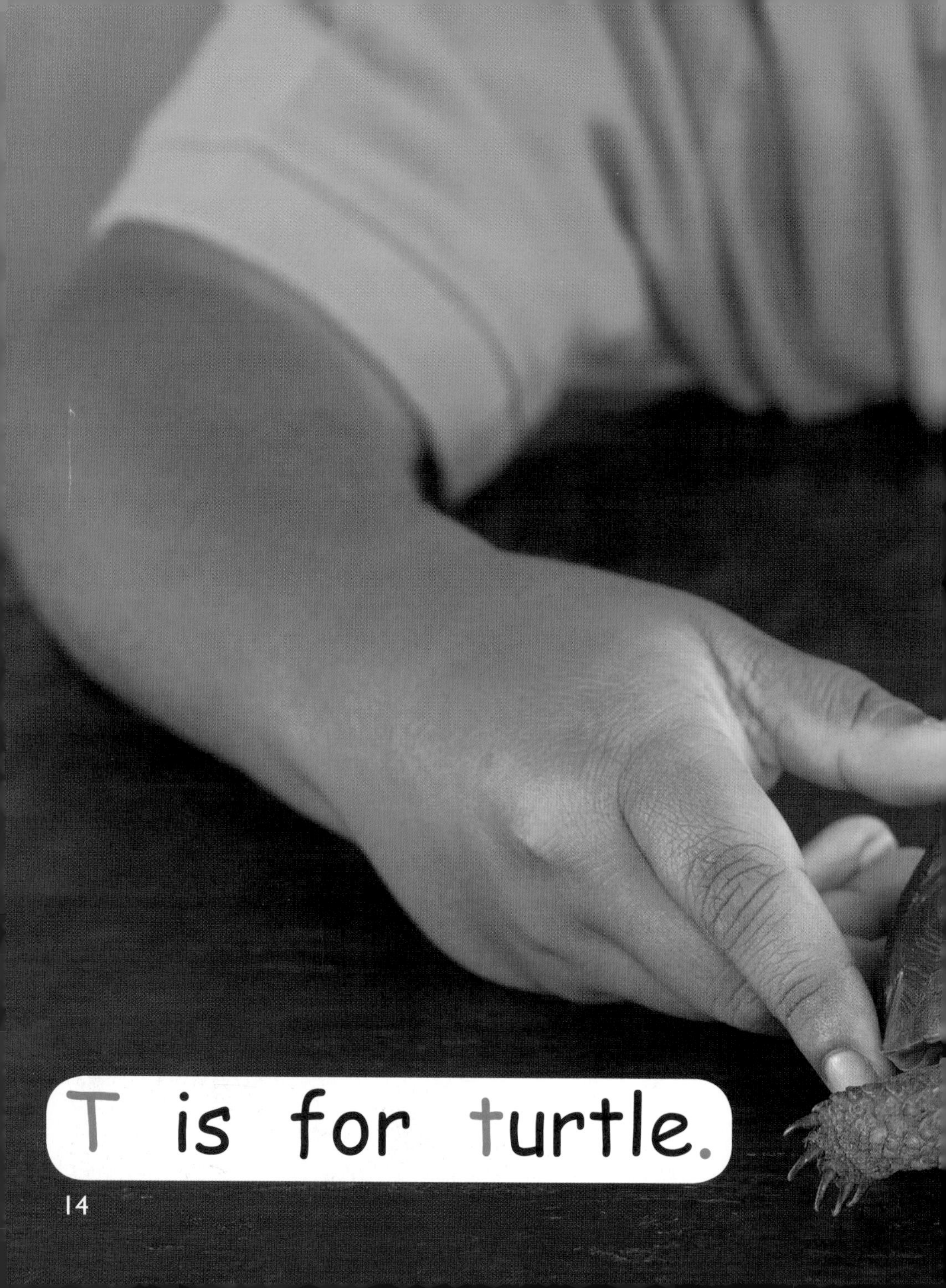

T is for turtle.

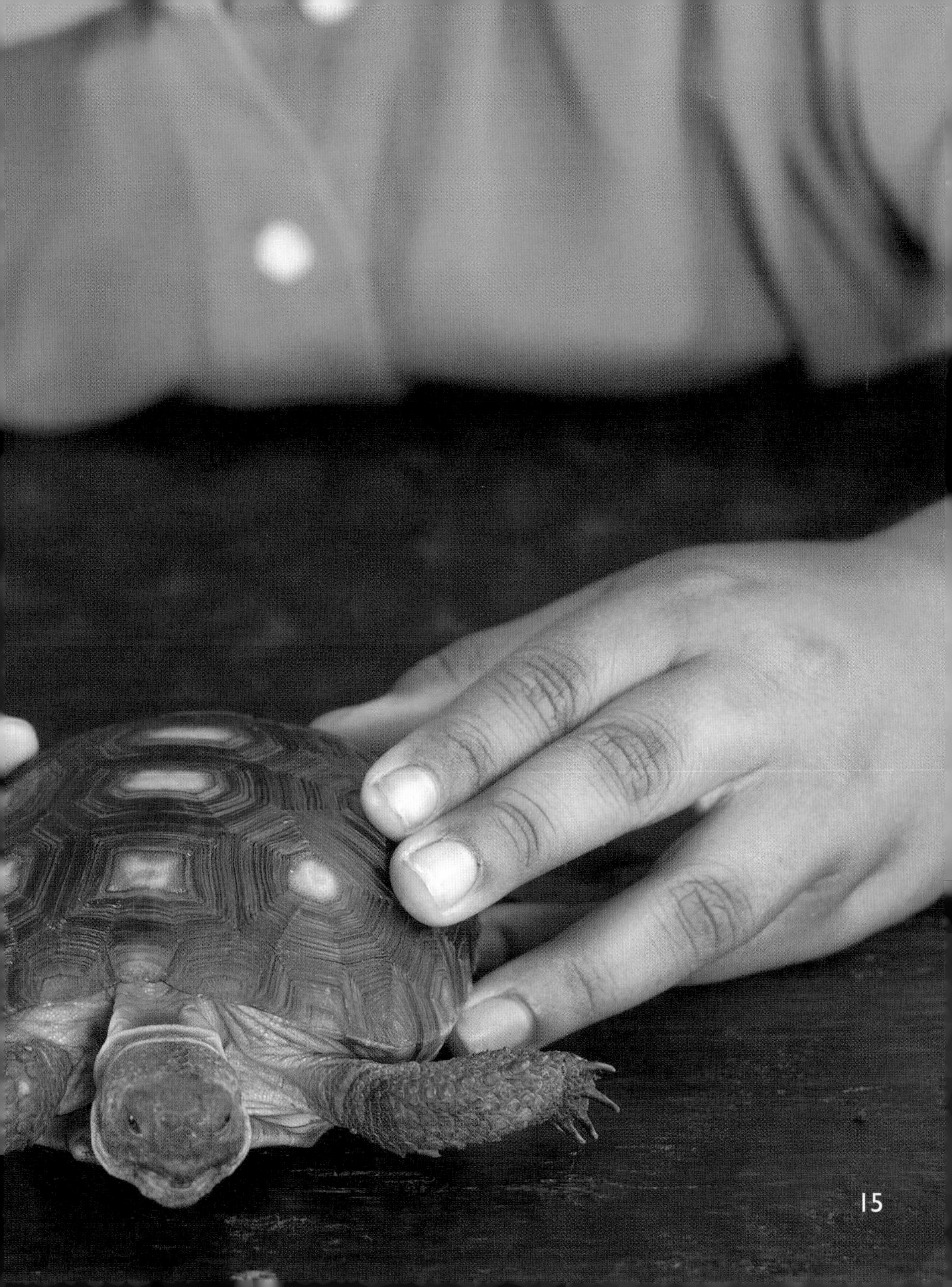

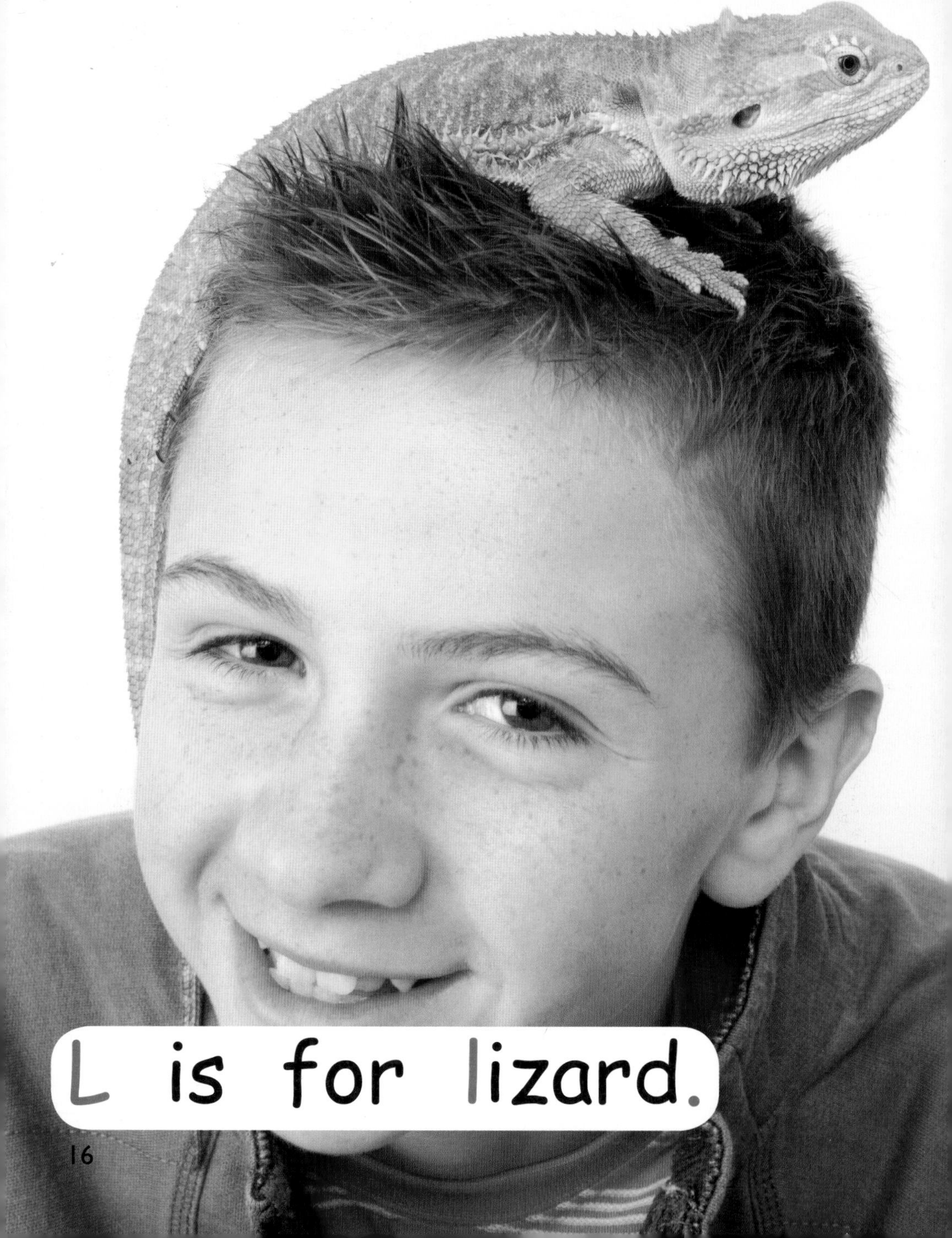

L is for lizard.